A REDNECK CHRISTMAS CAROL

Dickens Does Dixie

Illustrated by David Boyd

Adaptation by John Yow and T. Stacy Helton

LONGSTREET PRESS, INC.
Atlanta, Georgia

Published by
LONGSTREET PRESS, INC.
A subsidiary of Cox Newspapers
A subsidiary of Cox Enterprises, Inc.
2140 Newmarket Parkway, Suite 122
Marietta, GA 30067

Printed in the United States of America

1st printing 1997

Library of Congress Catalog Card Number: 97-71940

ISBN: 1-56352-429-5

Electronic film prep by OGI, Forest Park, GA
Cover art by David Boyd
Book design by Burtch Bennett Hunter

To my mother,
the only woman who's
loved me all of my life

— DAVID BOYD —

A REDNECK CHRISTMAS CAROL

Dickens Does Dixie

2

Euben Scrood was a real cheap man. Yankees might have called him a skinflint, foreigners might have called him a pennypincher, but the good folks of Sand Mountain, Alabama, particularly the people around Lake Water Moccasin, thought he was just cheap. And mean.

Euben was the owner of Eubie's Bait and Tackle, which he owned solo ever since his partner, Jake Marley, had that terrible accident. Even people who didn't like Eubie had to admit it was a great shop. You could get snuff, nickel hard-boiled eggs, beer, a muffler for a Ford pick-up (years '82 to '89), loaf bread, and motor oil all in one quick stop. Not to mention bait, lures, line, and poles.

Now Eubie had a fellow named Bobby Cratchet who had been working for him for three years. Bobby had married a Saunders from near Mobile, Nellie Jean, and the two of them had six children, none over the age of ten. Most men in Bobby's situation would love to be away from home, but not Bobby — he loved his kids, especially the youngest, little Timmy.

Decmber 24th was a lukewarm day on Lake Water Moccasin. The last of the fishermen had already visited Eubie's, snapping up the fancy new Repalla lures Eubie had imported all the way from Ft. Worth.

Bobby was stocking the snuff shelf when Eubie came in, eyeing Bobby and the unattended register. He also couldn't help noticing two jars of green tomato pickle on the countertop. And Eubie knew he didn't sell nothing in glass jars.

6

"Bobby, how many times I got to tell you never turn your back to the register. I don't pay you a teamster's wages to have every slack-jawed yokel steal me blind," Eubie fussed, making a beeline for the till.

"Sorry, Mr. Scrood. Just stocking the shelves, trying to get ahead. 'Cause you know, uh, tomorrow is . . ."

"And what's these durn tomatoes sittin' up here on the counter?"

"Well, uh, Big Ham Hammonds done left them there. He said . . ."

The sound of the register ringing open cut Bobby off. "I reckon I know what that old cuss said, but he better not think he can pay down his cash bill with no garden produce. Runs the biggest junk yard in the county and ain't parted with a dollar yet. Shoot, I could take lessons from Big Ham." Eubie stuffed the day's take in his pocket and then pushed the two jars down the counter toward Bobby.

"Here, you want these?" But then he stopped himself. "On second thought — maybe we can sell 'em for fifty cents apiece. And don't you be taking nothing off that sorry scoundrel's bill."

"Sure thing, Mr. Scrood. I'll put a price tag on them first thing tomorrow — I mean, day after tomorrow. 'Cause, uh, you know, tomorrow's . . ."

"Don't remind me . . . I'm gonna lose a day of business 'cause of Christmas. Seems like a sad state of affairs when the government can pick a man's pocket every 25th of December."

The weather was turning cool as Eubie left the bait shack, leaving Bobby to close down and put the nightcrawlers in the fridge. As he walked down the road into town, working a fresh chaw of Red Man and fingering the wad of bills in his pocket, he couldn't help shaking his head over all the dadgum idiots in the world — people who'd rather waste their time and throw their money away and act happy about it than keep their minds on getting ahead in the world. Idiots!

About the time he rounded the corner at the Tastee Freeze,

Eubie was approached by two men from the Pentecostal Church, Deacon Fritz and Deacon Weaver.

"Brother Eubie," Brother Fritz said, "can you spare some change for the po' kids and the empty stocking fund? That poor Jenkins family up near Bullseye was pretty near wiped out by that fire last Halloween."

"It was mighty sad," Brother Weaver added. "What with all those children left standing out in a freezing rain while their Daddy got himself killed trying to rescue all that stuff he still hadn't paid the taxidermist for."

Eubie stared at the two deacons like they were uttering jibberish from Swahililand. He didn't enjoy having people ask him for money.

"Brother Fritz, Brother Weaver, I pay taxes at the bait shop. I have to give Uncle Sam my money that I could be buying a new Evinrude motor with. I heard about that fire. . . started when their Momma passed out with a cigarette in her mouth, and no tellin' what all she'd been drinkin'. As far as those kids go, ain't there no more workfarms for the likes of them. . . ain't there no more welfare handouts? Why should I dip into my pocket to bail out all the sorry trash in the world?"

With that Eubie walked on down the road toward the Mercantile Bank. Deacons Fritz and Weaver just shook their heads.

Bobby Cratchett was mighty grateful that Eubie was giving him the day off. He loved Christmas and couldn't wait to spend it with his brood, even though with what Euben Scrood paid him there wouldn't be many presents for the children. One thing Bobby did have was a Christmas Dinner fit for the Mayor! Cranberry sauce from a can, a quart of creamed corn one of the kids had earned by cleaning out old lady Simpson's hen house, mashed potatoes, gravy, and the centerpiece — a little banty rooster that had wandered up into the yard a couple of months back.

Bobby locked up the door to the bait shack and turned around to find little Timmy right there waiting for him — sitting peaceful as a lamb on an old Yoohoo crate, with his gimpy leg stuck out and the little hickory crutch Bobby had made lying there beside him. Timmy started to stand up when his daddy came out, but before he could take a step Bobby came over and swung the boy up onto his shoulders and they headed off toward home — the two of 'em just happy as cows in clover.

Walking by the Barlow place, they stopped to watch Junior and Garnie, a couple of Barlow kids about Timmy's age, tormenting two fat sows in the hog pen — running after 'em and whipping at 'em with switches from a chinaberry tree, the boys hollering and the sows grunting just to beat the band.

"Aw, pappy," said Timmy, as Bobby set him down on the fence rail, "you reckon I'll ever be able to have that kind of fun again?"

"Course you will, Tim, and it won't be long," said Bobby. "But don't forget, running around barefoot in Uncle Grady's barn lot was how you got this dadburn hookworm in the first place."

D ark had settled in and a chilly wind was blowing by the time Eubie had made his way on out to the trailer park. A white moon threw spooky shadows from the big sweet-gum tree down across the dirt walkway leading up to his screen door, and Eubie felt a chill raise the hair on the back of his neck.

A sound like a dog howling made him jump as he tried to unlock his door, but he finally got inside and shut the door behind him. He threw the dead bolt and found the switch to the 20-watt lamp on the little table beside his chair.

19

Eubie had already eaten — stopped at the diner and spent sixty-five cents on a tuna fish sandwich, a lot of money but it was worth it not to have to worry about food again today.

He didn't want to turn on his little TV — one, because it would use more electricity, and two, because he knew the only thing on would be a bunch of idiots drooling over how wonderful Christmas was — so he was just sitting there in his chair when all of a sudden he heard somebody banging on his door.

'Bout scared the bejeezus out of him, but then he figured it was just some fool do-gooder lookin' for a donation. "Go away!" he hollered from where he sat. "If you're sellin' something, I don't want any, and if you're askin' for something, I ain't got any!" He was cackling to himself — right pleased at being so ornery — when the banging started up again.

He was about to holler out again, louder this time, when he heard his name being called, real low and mournful: "Euben Scrooooooood."

22

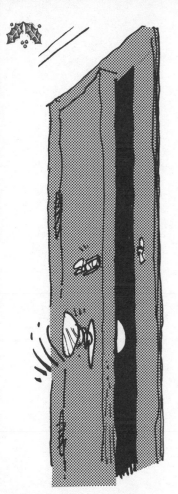

At the same time, as he stared at the door where the sound come from, danged if he didn't see the dead bolt just slidin' back all by itself.

He tried to holler "Great jumpin' Jehosophat!" but no sound came out of his mouth. He just kept starin', bug-eyed, as the door knob turned and the door began to creak open.

There before him stood a . . . a something . . . something standing up like a man, but also tangled up, one arm pinned across his chest and the other held straight down beside him. The John Deere cap on his head also looked tied down at a crazy angle, but Eubie couldn't tell just who it was standing there or what it was had him all snagged up on himself.

It reminded him of something, but he didn't know if it was from his real life or his worst dreams.

25

Eubie still sat there pressed back into his chair like Vienna sausage stuffed in a can, when the voice spoke again. "What's the matter, Eubie? You look like you seen a ghost."

With that, the strange figure started laughing like a demon from hell, doubled over, lost its balance — Eubie could see now its legs were bound together too — and fell headlong into the trailer.

"Gott dawgit, that hurt," said a voice that was just now starting to sound familiar.

With the light from the little lamp shining down on the figure on the floor, Eubie finally saw who it was paying him this visit.

"Jake, is that you?"

"None other, good buddy," said Jake Marley, trying to twist himself up into a sitting position.

"Well, what in the tarnation are you all tangled up in? Looks like fishing line. And what's that there hanging off your sleeve? Spinner bait?"

"These here are the lines and lures I wasted my whole life sellin'," said Jake, "and I'm here to try to make sure you don't make the same mistake."

"But Jake, ain't you dead? Didn't I see Lake Water Moccasin gobble you up like a frog on a gnat?"

"I'm dead, Eubie, deader'n a catfish in the deep-fryer. But I can't rest. I lived my whole life ass-backwards and now I got to pay for it."

"What you mean? We sold a heap of goods, kept that store open twelve hours a day seven days a week. What's wrong with that?"

"Naw, you don't understand, Eubie. But you will before this night's over. You're going to have a few more visitors — three to be exact — and they'll show you just what I'm talking about. Now, how 'bout helpin' me get back on my feet."

Well, ol' Eubie's about to decide he's been played for a fool, so he sits still for a minute, rubs his chin like he's thinking on something.

"I don't know, good buddy," he says. "Seems to me if you was a ghost, you could just fly right outta here. You wouldn't need no help."

Jake gives his head a slow, sorrowful shake. "I reckon you're right, Eubie. I don't need no help from the likes of you."

With that, Jake commenced to just up and disappear, a little at a time, from the feet upwards. By the time only his top half was left, Eubie's eyes had about popped out of his skull, and a couple of seconds later there wasn't nothin' left of Jake but his head — which still stared right back at Eubie. "One o'clock sharp," it said, then disappeared completely.

Eubie rubbed his eyes with the heels of his hands, then stared out again — nothing there. "Durned if there wasn't some bad mayo in that tuna fish."

It seemed like no sooner had Eubie got to sleep good than something woke him back up. Smoke! He threw off the covers and sat up quick, ready to make a run for it, when he found himself staring in the face of the biggest, ugliest woman he'd ever laid eyes on.

She was wearing a tank top big enough to cover an Oldsmobile 98, had her hair piled up in curlers and a Pall Mall hanging out the side of her mouth. She had pulled his kitchen chair up beside the bed and was just sitting right there looking at him. Behind the cigarette there was another smell — Handi-wipes.

33

"Don't ebm bother to ask, dipstick. I'm the first of the folks Jake told you was coming — the Ghost of Christmas Past — and I don't like this any better'n you do. But we got places to go and people to see." She hefted herself out of the chair and turned her backside to Eubie, squatted down a might, and said, "Hop on, cowboy, and let's ride."

"What about my clothes? I ain't wearing nothin' but this ol' Richard Petty t-shirt."

"Ain't noboby gonna see that scrawny butt, noway."

Once Eubie was situated on the spirit's back, his legs wrapped above her hips, arms around her neck — pretty durn comfy, really, kind of like riding a big old brood mare — the two of 'em just lifted right off the floor and went plumb through the roof of the trailer and out into the night sky.

In no time at all they were back to earth again, at the sight of Eubie's very first job: the corner of a truck garden on a wore-out farm outside of Chattanooga, 1960, where he and his best friend

Jake were digging for worms.

"Why'd you bring me here, Spirit?" asked Eubie. "I don't need to be reminded of back when I'd fight a dog off a chicken bone just to have something to eat."

The spirit lit up another Pall Mall and left it dangling while she answered: "What you need to be reminded of is that you wasn't always such a low-down, flint-hearted scoundrel."

Eubie watched the two boys at their work — himself and Jake all those years ago. The young Eubie broke open a clod of dirt and pulled out a big, fat wiggler, then held it up in front of Jake's face.

"Looky there," he whooped. "I believe I might have to use that one myself. Come on, Jake, let's take the rest of the afternoon off and do us a little fishing." He dropped the big worm into a Waffle House styrofoam cup.

"Hit ain't no way to get rich," said Jake. "But shoot."

Eubie stood silent as the two boys left their shovels and rakes lying there in the dirt and headed toward the shed where their cane poles were waiting. It was hard for him to remember now how he could have been so sorry and trifling — just leaving his work behind with no more thought than a jaybird. It wasn't but another year or two before him and Jake was stealing lumber from the future site of the new Freehope Baptist Church to build their first bait shack.

"Ain't I seen enough?" Eubie asked the spirit.

"You ain't got started yet. Climb aboard."

Next thing Eubie knew, he and the spirit were plopped on a couple of stools at one end of the soda fountain at Dixie Drugstore in Sand Mountain. The spirit pointed back over her shoulder with her thumb.

"I guess you know who that is."

Eubie spun his stool around a little ways and glanced into the booth behind him. Oh yeah, he knew who that was — Darlene Dobbins, about the prettiest little flower ever bloomed in north Alabama. But right this minute — wringing her napkin to shreds and glancing at the door every two seconds — she didn't look none too happy.

Just then the chime on the top of the door jingled and in hurried a young Euben Scrood. Eubie watched in fascination as this 20-year-old version of himself dropped into the booth opposite the lovely Darlene. An unpleasant memory was working its way up from the back of his mind.

"Eubie, I swan, I have been waiting here like a fool almost an hour. Why, it's too late to go to the show now. And just look at you!"

42

Well, he thought he looked like a working man ought to look: hair matted and sweaty, black grime rings around his neck, shirt and pants splattered with red dirt and cement mix, work boots covered with mud.

"Well, durn it, Darlene — me and Jake's got a business to run. We've just about got the new shack built out by the lake, and it ain't time to be thinking about no dadburn movie theater."

"I guess it ain't time to be thinking about me, neither," said Darlene, lighting up a Lucky and giving Eubie a hard look.

Eubie stared right back at her. "Matter a fact, no, it ain't. But Darlene, it won't always be like this. You got to loosen up on the choke-chain here for a while. Got to let this big dog run."

Darlene stubbed out her cigarette with a vengeance and stood up quick. "I'm gon' let you run, Mister — straight to blazes!" She grabbed up her purse and stomped right out, her ponytail bobbing behind her.

Perched on his stool, Eubie watched Eubie watch her go. Young Eubie looked like he made a move to go after her but then settled back down.

The spirit elbowed old Eubie in the side and blew a huge chest full of Pall Mall smoke in his face. "That right there's where you went wrong, bud-row. That girl ended up marrying one of Ernest Tubb's roadies. Done right well by herself. Now let's get you on home."

Eubie opened his eyes to find himself curled up on top of his bed with his pillow squeezed tight between his thighs. His first thought was that he'd had a terrible dream, but the thick haze of cigarette smoke — along with the crumpled-up Pall Mall pack on his little night table — made him realize the worst. Remembering Jake's promise that he'd have two more visitors before the night was over, Eubie jumped up and pulled on a pair of britches, then burrowed under his nappy, old bedspread and shut his eyes tight.

But it wasn't long before he heard the dreaded sound: "Euben Scrooooood."

Eubie peeked out from under the covers and saw a vision of pale blue polyester and rhinestone radiance. And hair, glossy black hair swept back like all get-out.

It couldn't be. But it had to be.

"Are you the . . . the King?" Eubie stuttered.

"Hankyuh, hankyuhveramuch, but no suh, I am not the King, not no longer. I am the Spirit of Christmas Present, come to show you what's going on on this fine Christmas morning. Now you just come along with me, boy."

He held open his cape — fringed with white rabbit fur, it looked like — and when Eubie walked over and stood beside him, the spirit wrapped him up and the world went dark.

The next thing Eubie saw was the little frame house that

belonged to his assistant, Bobby Cratchett. Eubie had seen the place lots of times, but the broken shutters, blistered old paint, and tar-paper roof had been easy enough to ignore. What Eubie had always noticed was the Dodge Challenger up on blocks in the yard. It had Yosemite Sam mudflaps on the back, and Eubie had often wondered how he could con Bobby out of them.

Eubie and the spirit glided up the front steps and into the house, where they were confronted by a scrawny pine tree with a ragdoll angel stuck to the top, more children than Eubie could count, and a foul smell that had to be cat pee. Eubie just hated cats.

"Take a real good look around," said the spirit. "Bobby may not have a bank vault full of money like you got, but he's doing pretty doggone good in the family department."

"I dunno," Eubie said, thinking how glad he was he didn't have all them durn children running around his place. He couldn't stand the thought of sticky, clumsy kids' hands fiddling with his Elvis whiskey decanters, his Confederate checkers set (blue and gray mock-marble pieces), or his NASCAR coffee mugs.

The Cratchett family was just sitting down to Christmas dinner. The vegetables were already steaming on the table, along with a plate of loaf bread, when Mrs. Cratchett came in carrying a covered platter. She set it down in front of Bobby and removed the cover with a flourish.

The whole family started oohing and ahing while Eubie peered over at the sorriest looking little roasted bird he'd ever seen. He wondered if it might be a durn bob-white.

Meanwhile, little Timmy got up from his seat and hobbled down to the end of the table to get a better look at the thing.

"Why ain't Bobby done nothin' to help that boy?" Eubie whispered to the spirit, who had grabbed himself a piece of bread and dipped it in the gravy.

"Eubie, that pore man's got a sight more to worry about than little Timmy's hookworm. Where's he gonna get money for medicine? You don't pay him nothin' and then you turn around and tax that." The spirit licked his fingers clean. "Lordy, what I wouldn't give for a fried peanut butter sandwich right now."

The ghost was about to stick his finger in the bowl of mashed potatoes when Bobby held up his hand to hush the kids. "Children, it's time for the blessing."

With the room all of a sudden quiet as a junkyard in January, Bobby began: "Dear Lord God, we give thanks with all our hearts for all your blessings — for this fine Christmas morning, for the love that we share with You and with each other, and for your Son who died to save us from the eternal flames. And also Lord, we give thanks for Mr. Euben Scrood, who made this wonderful feast possible."

Hearing these words, Eubie hiked his britches up and gave the spirit a big ol' grin.

54

"Amen!" said the family at the end of Bobby's fine blessing. But before anybody could strap on the feed bag, Mrs. Cratchett spoke up.

"That's mighty good of you to include Mr. Scrood, honey, but I'll tell you what — if that sorry son of a she-dog was here right this minute, I dang sure would give him something besides a blessing. That flint-tipped tightwad is the very reason little Timmy here is walking around with one leg curled up under him. You couldn't pry honest pay out of that gutless geezer with a crowbar and a can of motor oil. There, I've done had my say. Now let's eat."

Figuring that Eubie had heard what he needed to hear, the spirit swept him up in his cape and flew him on back home and set him down on his bed.

"Well, ain't that a fine howdy-do," Eubie whined. "Here's a pore dumb peckerwood, got a zillion kids but nary a bread crumb to throw at 'em. I give him a job and put food on his table, and what do I get? Cussed out by that scraggledy-haired witch. Now tell me, Spirit, am I missin' somethin' here?"

The spirit was over rummaging around in Eubie's little Frigidaire but not finding anything that hadn't already turned into something else. He closed the door and moved back over beside the bed.

"Yeah, Eubie," he said, "you're missing something. But you're about to find it, you sorry ol' hound dog."

With that, the spirit wrapped himself up in his cape and disappeared in a wisp of powder-blue smoke.

This time Eubie didn't even try to go to sleep. He just lay there on his back, eyes open, still as a gravestone, waiting to hear his name called out. But this one came quiet. It was a darkness falling over him, and it 'bout scared the whiskers right off Eubie's face. He looked up beside the bed and saw a giant — seven, eight feet tall — wrapped up in a shroud black as midnight. There was a hood over its head, but where there should have been a face, danged if there wasn't a lit up mask of Jimmy Carter, just grinning to beat the band.

The spirit didn't say a word, just lifted what looked like an empty black sleeve and gestured toward the door. Eubie rose from the bed, and the next thing he knew, he and the spirit were standing in the middle of a sprawling junk car graveyard — Big Ham's Auto Salvage. Cars and pieces of cars stacked on top of one another as far as the eye could see.

"Spirit," cried Eubie, "why in Jake's blazes have you brought me here? The man that runs this place is my sworn enemy."

The spirit lifted its sleeve to point to a pile of cars a little ways off to Eubie's left. It looked like the car on top had toppled off and was lying upside down next to the others.

Actually, Eubie recognized the car. It was — or had been — a perfectly restored 1966 GTO 389 tri-power with 450 horses and a four speed, and it was Little Ham's pride and joy; that is, until he double-flipped it off of U.S. 81 while running some contraband for his daddy. Little Ham had walked away from the accident, but, from a mental standpoint, the boy just hadn't been right since losing that car. But who could blame him? Wasn't a man in the whole county older than twelve didn't covet that car — including Euben Scrood.

It wasn't a pretty sight for Eubie, upside down like that and crumpled like a durn accordion. But the spirit was drawing him closer and closer, until his eyes finally lit on the two feet sticking out from underneath the wreck.

61

Well, what in the tarnation, thought Eubie. Something about them cheap, imitation snakeskin boots looked mighty familiar. "Spirit," he rasped, "who is this pore dead son of a gun?"

The spirit lifted his black sleeve slowly, and the side of the car rolled up with it, revealing the dirty jeans, the big Winston Cup belt buckle, the frayed "No Fat Chicks" t-shirt . . .

Eubie's stomach turned slap over and he hid his eyes from the dreadful sight. The spirit allowed the car to ease on back down.

"But how?" pleaded Eubie. "Why?"

The spirit's sleeve pointed to the ground a few feet away, where a lug wrench and a wheel key lay in the dirt.

Then Eubie looked at the GTO's mag wheels, still gleaming like treasure after all the car had been through. He didn't need to ask no more questions. He could see himself plain enough, scrambling up that stack of junk to steal the wheels off Little Ham's prized possession — and the picture in his mind didn't sit none too well.

Well, there was one more question: "Spirit," he asked, reaching out at the empty sleeve, "what you've showed me here, is it somethin' that's bound to happen or somethin' that just might happen?"

The only answer he got was darkness coming down.

Sunlight poured in the little roll-out window over his bed and splashed right across Eubie's face. He opened his eyes into it and for a minute thought he'd been struck blind. But when he raised his hands to shade his eyes, he realized he could see after all. And if he could see, that meant he probably wasn't dead either.

He jumped out of bed — still wearing his britches and t-shirt — pulled on his boots and his old khaki fishing shirt and went running out of the trailer. First person he saw was Maudie Tompkins sitting on the stoop of the trailer next door smoking a cigarette. Looked like she had a new set of curlers in her hair.

"Miss Maudie," he hollered, "what day is it?"

"What dad-blamed day you think it is, fool. It's Christmas Day."

I'm not too late, he said to himself as he ran for his truck. I haven't missed it.

Ten minutes later he was skidding to a stop in front of Big Ham's weather-beaten frame house and sending a couple of Rhode Island Reds squawking up onto the open front porch. Eubie did his best to toot "Jingle Bells" on the horn of the Ford Ranger.

Finally Big Ham came through the screen door, barefoot, wearing a long-sleeve undershirt and a pair of overalls. He was eating what looked to Eubie like a piece of pecan pie — it couldn't be but 8:15 in the morning.

"Merry Christmas, Big Ham," boomed Eubie as he slid down out of the cab of his truck.

"I can't believe even a no-good skinflint like you would be out collectin' on Christmas morning," said Ham. He picked the wedge of pie up off the paper plate and took another big bite. "How much I owe you?"

Eubie looked up at the man who out-talled him by a good eight inches and outweighed him by twice. "Oh, I'd say about two quarts of green tomato pickle worth. Best I ever tasted, by the way."

"I'll tell the wife you said so. But let me get this straight: you're saying them two jars of 'maters settles our bill right down to zero?

What's that connivin' little mind of yourn got cooked up?"

"Well, now that you mention it, I do need to ask a favor."
Big Ham dropped the paper plate on the floor of the porch for the chickens to peck at the pie crumbs. "What is it?" he asked.

"You got a turkey hangin' in your smokehouse?"

"Got a nice, fat hen I shot some time after Thanksgiving."

"What you want for it?"

"Well, let's just say my bill stood right at two quarts of 'mater pickle and one fat turkey. It is Christmas, I reckon."

What else, what else? Eubie asked himself as he raced back toward town. The fat smoked turkey on the seat beside him was good, especially for Bobby and the Missus, but what about all them durn kids?

Then it hit him. He screeched to a stop, turned around in the middle of the road and sped out to the bait shack. Candy! Why, he had shelves full of it.

He ran into the shack, pulled out his biggest grocery sack, and commenced to fill it up: Moon Pies, Goo Goo Clusters, Baby Ruths, Fireballs, bubblegum, M&Ms, Three Musketeers, Kit Kats. Shoot, he had it all.

Eubie glanced around the room as soon as Bobby Cratchett opened the door. The kids were sitting on the floor, and it looked like they were going through their Christmas stockings. From what he could see, each one had gotten either an apple or an orange along with a handful of walnuts. Eubie grinned like a mule eating briars.

He lay the turkey down on the table where Mrs. Cratchett sat holding little Timmy in her lap. "Something to put in your oven on this fine Christmas Day."

"Why, bless your heart, Euben Scrood," replied Mrs. Cratchett.

"And if it ain't too far out of line," Eubie continued, still beaming, and still holding the bulging grocery sack in his left arm, "I got a little surprise for the children, too."

He stepped over to the middle of the room, bent down, and slowly emptied the sack onto the floor. It made quite a pile, if he did say so.

The kids just sat there bug-eyed, mouths wide
open. They looked up at Eubie, then at their
father. Bobby looked at Eubie, Eubie
grinned and nodded, and the children
went at that pile like bees on honeycomb.

Eubie took Bobby by the elbow and
steered him toward the door. "If you'll
just step outside with me for a minute,"
he said, "there's something I need to ask."

Bobby was still right dumb-
founded by the whole sit-
uation as he let Eubie lead him
out into the yard.

Eubie motioned toward the old Dodge up on blocks beside the house. "D'I ever tell you how much I admire them mudflaps you got on that Challenger?"

"Uh, no, no sir," Bobby stuttered, "but they's yours for the askin'."

"Well, thank you kindly," said Eubie. "'Cause you see, Bobby, I just love cars and all the trimmins that go with 'em, and I been thinkin' — I might be inclined to expand that part of my bidness, maybe lease a whole nother building. In which case I'd need a partner to take over the bait shack. What you think?"

"A partner?" Bobby crowed. "Why, Mr. Scrood, I don't know what to say."

"Well, I guess you can start by saying 'Eubie' instead of that 'Mr.' nonsense."

75

"But Mr. Scr . . . Eubie! Eubie, Eubie, this is my dream come true, my Christmas wish. Bless you, Eubie, bless you."

Eubie walked over to his truck, then turned back to Bobby as he opened the door.

"You, too, Bobby, and your wife and your children. May the good Lord bless ever durn one of us."